The Spirit of DEMOCRATIC CAPITALISM

THIRTY YEARS LATER

MICHAEL NOVAK

ISBN-978-0-578-16399-4

Published by The Institute for Faith, Work & Economics
8400 Westpark Drive
Suite 100
McLean, Virginia 22102

www.tifwe.org

Printed in the United States of America

In partnership with

the M.J. Murdock Charitable Trust,

celebrating 40 years of

working for the common good.

Foreword

by Anne R. Bradley

In 1982 Michael Novak changed the minds of many people, particularly Christians, about the moral and economic benefits of capitalism with his iconic book, *The Spirit of Democratic Capitalism*. At that time, we didn't know that the Soviet experiment with central planning would come to an end, and we were nearing the end of one of the bloodiest centuries in human history. The year 1982 was a time in which the world was waiting to see the direction of history and whether capitalism could survive and even thrive in the face of totalitarian and authoritarian regimes that populated the globe.

Thirty years later, we know that we stand on the positive side of history. The Soviet experiment came to a crumbling end, and economic freedom and political freedom have made great strides across the planet. It would not be an understatement to assert that Michael Novak played a large role in helping leaders and citizens in many countries understand the virtues necessary for a flourishing society, and that democratic capitalism paved the road to greater possibilities for democratic institutional reform and liberal moral values.

In terms of helping people escape from tyranny and authoritarianism which thwart our God-given impulse to unleash creativity, we still have progress to make. Latin America is falling to socialism and more central planning experiments, most of the Middle East remains economically and politically unfree, and where China is headed remains a question of cautious optimism.

As Christians, we know that we must help bring about greater levels of flourishing and care for the vulnerable. The most effective way to do this is with market-based societies and democratic institutions. This short book by Michael Novak is a retrospective commentary on his former, iconic book and reveals that we must pursue freedom and we must remain vigilant if we want the reform we so desperately seek for people around the world.

The Spirit of Democratic Capitalism: Thirty Years Later

It is not often that a new form of political economy appears in history, fills a need, and takes root in universal discourse. When I first showed a prospective publisher the title of *The Spirit of Democratic Capitalism* (1982),[1] he objected to the word "capitalism" in the title. It was a term of such denigration, he thought, as to have become irredeemable. To alter the title, I demurred, would have been to accept a falsely contrived definition of the term. It would have been to surrender without a fight. The point is that those who in each generation disparage capitalism mean by "capitalism" something quite false—in fact, so out of touch with reality that they should be ashamed. For instance, they define capitalism as constituted by three things: the market, private property, and private profit. The Soviet idea of socialism entailed the abolition of all three. But those three are not the essence of capitalism. Instead, they designate the traditional economy known from the beginning of civilization.

My plan for this chapter is to begin with the definitional issue, then to discuss the immense changes in political economies of the world during the past thirty years or so. After that, I describe the case of democratic capitalism in the United States, which is constituted by laws and systems that regulate and support the dynamism of creativity and invention. I conclude with reflections on the fragility of free societies, the driving question of how best to help the poor, and the underlying biblical inspirations of democratic capitalism.

The Definitional Issue

The definition of capitalism offered in virtually every English-language dictionary is decidedly flat. See *Merriam-Webster*, for instance:

> an economic system characterized by private or corporate ownership of capital goods, by investments that are determined by private decision, and by prices, production, and the distribution of goods that are determined mainly by competition in a free market.[2]

What I propose, however, is a more dynamic understanding of capitalism:

> the invention-based economic system made possible by laws protecting intellectual property, plus personal habits of economic initiative, enterprise, and practical wisdom, and in which the main cause of wealth is fresh ideas, ventures, and exercised know-how.

Further, I would add that capitalism replaces both the agrarian economy, in which the chief source of wealth is land, and the mercantile economy, in which the chief source of wealth is international shipping and trade. It is also useful to distinguish capitalism from socialism by noting their asymmetry: socialism is the name of a dream in which political, economic, and cultural authorities are centralized in one unified system, whereas capitalism designates only the economic system, ordered by both separate and independent political and cultural systems.

Capitalism thus understood refers to a new system that came fully into being in the eighteenth century, one *whose results are exactly opposite* to many projections. Marx said its effect would be the immiseration of the poor.[3] Adam Smith used the term "universal opulence" to describe the aim of the system he identified in its early beginnings, and of course in the title of his great book, he spoke of the wealth of *nations*, not individuals, and explicitly included Africa and the Americas (South and North) in his discussions.[4] Smith identified new inventions and new and enterprising ideas as the chief cause of t*he creation of steadily greater wealth among all nations.* He also pointed out how in North America, wealth was being created from the bottom up, from the small farms, resulting in the capital funds that over time built the factories that produced previously unavailable goods. The central idea of capitalism is that wealth is created by insight, know-how, and discovery, as in Smith's illustration of the pin machine. Universal wealth is best created not by slavery or serfdom, and not by governmental direction from the top down, but by free women and free men using their own inventive and industrious minds to serve the largest public they can reach.

To reiterate: What I mean by "capitalism," and what capitalism really is, is a new economic system that arose in history, ripening at about the end of the 1700s, not known in its full form to the ancient, medieval, or even early modern world. It is considerably more than a market system, or a system of private property, or a system of private accumulation of profits. All those features belong to ancient systems, medieval systems, pre-modern and traditional systems. In the biblical period, there was certainly *private property*; otherwise "Thou shalt not steal" (Exodus 20:15, KJV) made little sense. Jerusalem was nothing but a *marketplace* at the juncture of three continents; it became modestly rich neither by industry nor by fertile agriculture. And *profits* became gifts that contributed to the building of the glorious temple. So these three characteristics—property, markets, and private profits—by no means define what was new about the modern system of economy lately christened "capitalism." (By the way, *private* profits are often invested soon in *public* companies contributing to the common good, making widely available inexpensive breakfast cereal, for example.)

During most of the time in which the aforementioned earlier systems flourished, the economic world was virtually static. Not much changed from the time of Christ until the late eighteenth century. Only

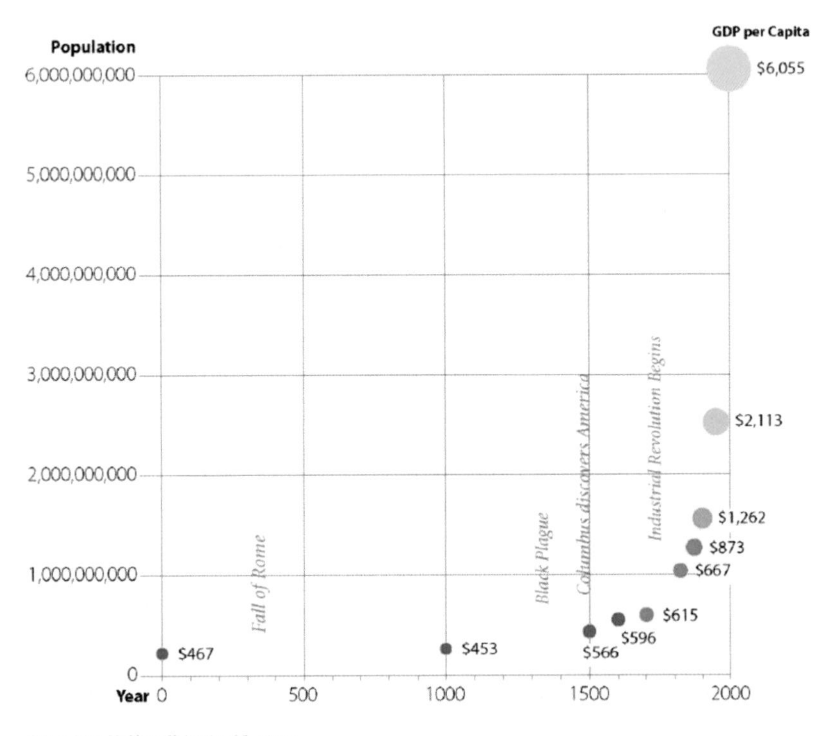

then, at about the year 1800, did the economic wealth of the world's population shoot almost straight upward from the virtual flatline of all prior history. See, for example, the following chart:[6]

A further important clarification: The term *capitalism* by itself fails to capture the full range of effects of the new system which Smith referred to as the new "system of natural liberty." Indeed, the new economy modified the traditional forms of *polity* and sharply spurred the demand for popular representation. It also promoted the building of new *cultures* by giving wider scope to commerce and especially to the gift of invention. A new political ideal was born: that of the commercial republic. Such a republic called for new virtues of civic republicanism: the seizing of personal responsibility and new habits

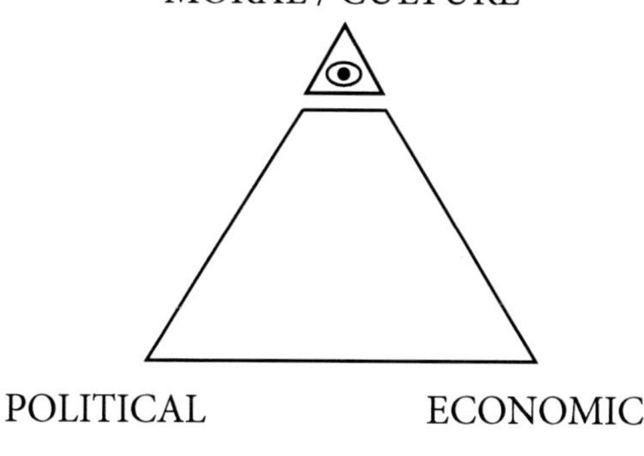

THE NEW ORDER OF THE AGES

of self-government both in private and in public life. In brief, the new system had not only an economic dimension but also political and cultural dimensions as well. This new system is best illustrated by a triangle, for these three dimensions—political, economic, and cultural—are all essential to a proper understanding of capitalism.

Given the long grip on the imagination of older models of polity, economy, and culture in Europe, the full scope of the new system could not be grasped. It was at first announced under the name *Novus Ordo Seclorum* on the Great Seal of the United States and dated MDCCLXXVI. It could not be grasped, in fact, for another two generations, until Alexis de Tocqueville had the brilliant idea of going to investigate these novelties for himself. He reported his early findings in *Democracy in America* (1835, 1840).[8]

In the eighteenth century, a host of thinkers had established the more complex term "political economy" to add to the traditional subject matter of Aristotle's *Politics*. At least these two terms are required to express the complex social system required for human liberty and flourishing: not just politics alone. For human liberty and human flourishing are fulfilled by neither politics alone nor economics alone. Rather, they require economic activity within a free polity, under the rule of law, and through the daily practice of personal habits of wisdom and self-control. Madison, Hamilton,

Jefferson, and their colleagues referred to the intellectual movement that led to this new conception as the new science of politics. Unlike all previous thinkers who had written on such affairs, these thinkers recognized the need for the larger concept of political economy.

When I proposed the idea of "democratic capitalism" in the 1980s, it was as a new name for the sort of political economy that characterized the free world, and toward which many of the unfree were now willing to work, a political economy of full human flourishing. Democratic capitalism means a system of natural liberty, requiring both political liberty and economic liberty — but also more. Prior those two is the acute need for a particular moral and cultural system, constituted by both new institutions and new personal habits. True liberty must be derived from self-control, and such liberty is best ordered by laws. Hence the need for a third science, the science of *moral ecology*, to discern all the institutions and personal moral habits essential for the flourishing of self-governing peoples. Under this view, liberty does not mean freedom from all restraints; rather, liberty means ordering one's own life—that is, self-government—for the sake of full human flourishing, through reflection and deliberation. Democratic capitalism, therefore, is a system of three liberties: political liberty, economic liberty, and liberty in religion and conscience, in arts and in science, and in cultural expression. (For brevity's sake, I call this third sphere of liberty moral/cultural liberty).

Without due attention to the interactions among these three systems, arguments pitched against democratic capitalism fall like arrows short of their target. Those vital interactions are the whole point of the concept and of the united "system of three systems" that it represents.

During the thirty years since this threefold system was first put forth, many critics have attacked it only in amputated form. Some think of it as no more than a libertarian system, concerned with economic liberty only, exaggeratedly individualistic, indifferent or even antithetical to welfare programs for the poor, unconcerned with the public good, focused solely on markets and private profit. Others think of it as libertarian mainly in the moral sense: pivoting solely on the ego of the individual (as in the thought of Ayn Rand), her pleasures, her contentment, her will-to-power. But in truth the criteria of democratic capitalism require attention to all three dimensions of human flourishing: economic, political, and moral/cultural. This threefold complexity may be fancifully suggested by the flags of free societies. Typically they have three colors, as if to signal the complexities of a full concept of liberty. This illustration is fanciful, but its vividness may help the mind grasp the threefold system in one.

Tremendous Effects Around the World

During the past three decades, tremendous changes have taken place in the political economy of more than a hundred nations. When Ronald Reagan took office in 1981, the huge populations of China and the Soviet Union had communist political economies, and India was governed under a Fabian (mildly) socialist economy.[10] The majority of the rest of the world lived under fairly fierce dictatorships, including most of Latin America, Africa, Southeast Asia, Eastern and Central Europe, North Korea, Cuba, and nearly all of the Middle East except Israel.

My own reconsiderations about political economy began before the Reagan administration, at a time when the Carter administration still hoped to serve two full terms. The previous Democratic nominee for president, George McGovern (in whose presidential campaign I eagerly served), was even further to the left than Carter. Both McGovern and Carter pointed to *inequality* as the main theme they would focus on. Old warriors like me well remembered McGovern's proposed "demogrants"[11] for wealth redistribution and Carter's war against inegalitarian horrors such as three-martini lunches.

During the 1980s, most of the communist and socialist nations of the world were already quietly dropping their failed economic systems and turning to markets, private property, and personal enterprise. Why? Because one system didn't work and the other did. India started the tide, the Chinese saw its success, and the Soviet nations saw themselves as wrongly deprived. Meanwhile, in this country, during the Carter years, Keynesian policies led to previously unheard-of "stagflation"[12] and economic malaise. During the four Carter years, ever-growing inflation wiped out a third of the value of those on fixed incomes, throwing millions into poverty.

Whether capitalism or socialism is a better system for dramatically reducing poverty was thus a well-settled question by the mid-1980s. As I wrote in *The Spirit of Democratic Capitalism*, the most underreported fact of the twentieth century was the death of socialism. It was dead, all right, but that underreported death would take a little more time to become overpoweringly evident to all. The global turn toward capitalism began not long after, in 1989, and within 25 years some 2 billion people had begun moving from communism and socialism toward capitalism, and thence out of poverty and into steadily advancing standards of living. These numbers were most notable in China, India, and the former Soviet Union and its captive nations.

By 2008, the world's population had risen to roughly 7 billion people, most of them living longer than ever before, through the blessing of sophisticated new medicines pioneered in advanced capitalist countries. Today there are still about a billion more persons who need to be raised up out of poverty. Succeeding in this project is the number-one moral priority of our time.

If I may repeat an important point made earlier, Adam Smith called his book *An Inquiry into the Nature and Causes of the Wealth of Nations* (1776)—nations, not individuals. The task laid out in that book is a social mission, not an individualist one, and it will not be completed until all nations and all persons are included within the upward sweep of the inventive economy.

I started to write about democratic capitalism in the 1970s in an effort to explain to my overseas friends (and to myself) just what the American new order is (i.e., What is this *Novus Ordo Seclorum?*). One could not learn this simply by reading the political philosophers and political scientists, who didn't write much about economics or culture. Nor could it be learned by reading only the economists, who for the most part wrote not nearly enough about the polity, the presence (or absence) of the rule of law, natural rights, and a culture of creativity. Nor did the literary figures and humanists seem to explore the new model of society in which it was their privilege to dwell (a society with heretofore "no model on the face of the globe," as Madison put it in *Federalist* 14 [13]). Therefore, it seemed, a lot of work remained to be done to put into words the nature of our tripartite system: a culture, a polity, an economy—all three in a distinctive framework of checks and balances, and obligated to respect the natural rights of every man and woman and the common good. Blessedly, our founders stressed three terms with not quite identical meanings: the public interest, public good, or general welfare. They also recognized, with originality among political actors, the debilitating daily consequences of human sin (often overlooked by utopians), desperately in need of constant, vigilant correction.

The underlying anthropology of the *Novus Ordo* held that there is enough sin in humans to make the survival of liberty problematic, but also enough *virtue* to give a regime of liberty a chance, albeit a precarious chance. It might even be necessary to merely muddle through. The survival of free regimes in this world is not guaranteed. The free society in each of its three systems must remain morally healthy itself, and then its three systems must remain in healthy balance with one another. A society composed of a threefold system of liberties lives always in danger of suicide, always in danger of pulling its moral foundations out from under itself. Is that contingency a biblical vision, or what?

Democratic Capitalism in the United States

Each of the three systems of democratic capitalism depends on the other two. The *economy* cannot work without a *polity* of law respectful of natural rights, as well as the cultural habits or virtues necessary to support all three systems-in-one. The polity cannot work without the habits of the heart which respect both the ordinances of the law and the rights of every other person in the political system. These habits constitute a culture of civic republicanism. And the *culture* can barely survive under a hostile economic system driven by cupidity, envy, smothering control by the state, or personal moral heedlessness. Nor can it survive under a hostile polity contemptuous of truth, justice, law, and beauty. Further, this culture will fall into lassitude and nihilism unless it maintains its longing for the transcendent, its upward thrust into the future, and the highest aspirations of the human heart. As Tocqueville saw, without that upward thrust, belief in the inviolable dignity of every single person will not survive, nor will respect for truth in public discourse. Belief in immortality and the certainty of divine judgment are indispensable supports of public virtue, our founders thought. Sheer materialism will suck the breath out of the human spirit.

In other words, an economy without beauty, love, human rights, respect for one another, civic friendship, and strong families (the tutors of moral habits) is not likely long to be loved, or to survive, or to be worthy of human persons. Those who focus almost exclusively on markets or even enterprise do not wholly capture the American system as it has functioned ever since the beginning. Ours is not a country of individualists; it is a country of joiners, country dances, church picnics, committees for every kind of purpose, a community of communities. Our people are typically communitarian individuals with sustained, time-consuming efforts at building local communities, organizing counties, ratifying independent states, forming a continental Union. If one looks into the history of America's small towns along the westward expansion of the country (such as in my wife's Iowa), the daily virtues, habits, and cooperative ventures of the pioneers (laboring together to put up churches, schools, and each other's homes) stun the mind. Americans build associations for every project that comes before them. They call for new committees to be formed with every project they face. When has there ever been a people who volunteer to attend so many meetings, or publish so many newsletters, or contribute to so many fundraisers? No civil society has ever been so thick with social activities. Even those who call themselves individualists or libertarians erect their own associations.

As noted above, what constitutes the essence of capitalism is the spirit and practice of creativity: invention, discovery, using one's head. Such gifts are exercised through new institutions. One such is the patent and copyright clause of section 8 of the first article of the U.S. Constitution. Abraham Lincoln called this clause one of the six most important steps in the history of liberty. It displaced the main form of the world's wealth from land and its fruits to the inventions of mind, from farming, fishing and hunting to intellectual property. It jolted humans out of the agrarian age (which goes back nearly to the beginning of civilization) into the Age of Invention.

Virtually every business and industry in the United States today is based upon a new insight into the creation and distribution of goods and services. Furthermore, the greater the number of people who are served, the wealthier the society (and also the inventor) may become. This is a pedestrian and humble system, but it serves the common good better than any other along some important dimensions, using a device that gives incentives to inventors, discoverers, and creative persons in almost all fields. In this humble way the about-to-become-wealthy are led to serve many (not all) elements of the common good. Incentives drive them to serve more and more people. This incentive system is not the perfect ideal that purists might wish. Yet Pope John Paul II in *Centesimus Annus* (1991) praised the happy chance of having both the interests of the common good and the interests of the human person served in one fell swoop:

> Moreover, man, who was created for freedom, bears within himself the wound of original sin, which constantly draws him towards evil and puts him in need of redemption. Not only is *this doctrine an integral part of Christian revelation*; it also has great hermeneutical value insofar as it helps one to understand human reality. Man tends towards good, but he is also capable of evil. He can transcend his immediate interest and still remain bound to it. The social order will be all the more stable, the more it takes this fact into account and does not place in opposition personal interest and the interests of society as a whole, but rather seeks ways to bring them into fruitful harmony.[15]

And John Paul II pointed out that, although held in low esteem by aristocrats and artists, business corporations give a role to individual persons working in a productive enterprise that the church has always taught: both the person and the association are mutually needed for the human fulfilment of each, and also to serve the good of the human race. John Paul II wrote:

> It is precisely the ability to foresee both the needs of others and the combinations of productive factors most adapted to satisfying those needs that constitutes another important source of wealth in modern society. . . . [M]any goods cannot be adequately produced through the work of an isolated individual; they require the cooperation of many people in

> working towards a common goal. Organizing such a productive effort, planning its duration in time, making sure that it corresponds in a positive way to the demands which it must satisfy, and taking the necessary risks—all this too is a source of wealth in today's society. . . .
> This process, which throws practical light on a truth about the person which Christianity has constantly affirmed, should be viewed carefully and favourably. Indeed, besides the earth, man's principal resource is *man himself.* His intelligence enables him to discover the earth's productive potential and the many different ways in which human needs can be satisfied. It is his disciplined work in close collaboration with others that makes possible the creation of ever more extensive *working communities* which can be relied upon to transform man's natural and human environments.[16]

To sum up, capitalism is the mind-centered system, springing from the creative power of insight, invention, and discovery. As we observe in the case of America, this new system is constituted by laws and institutions that regulate and support the dynamism of creativity and invention. These include such things as the patent and copyright clause, as well as institutions of venture capital, credit unions, and other investment houses. Sources of investment capital are indispensable because the movement from a creative idea to actual production requires a great deal of borrowing, the more so if the inventor is without personal wealth. Therefore, interest rates need to be reasonably low, secure, and reliable for both borrower and lender. The right of new businesses to obtain legal incorporation as a business is also crucial. This power does not naturally or necessarily belong to the state; but for good order, the state does have an interest in registering incorporations in a publicly available method.

Open markets are not the essence of capitalism, but they are an important social institution. They allow for new products, even entirely new industries, to be presented to the public for examination and rejection or purchase. The competition thus induced brings down prices, as newer products offer more attractive features or even wholly new possibilities, as we have observed in the development of computers, smartphones, digital cameras, medical devices of all sorts, and genetic therapies. At first these products are too expensive for you and me. But successes attract imitators and rivals. Competing products come into existence to please a wider range and variety of buyers. In this way, products at first complex and expensive and available only to the rich, rather quickly come down in price; they steadily expand to reach the mass market and to become available even to the poor. In 2005 in the United States, for instance, 64 percent of poor households had cable or satellite television, and 38 percent had a personal computer. [17] Just twenty-five years earlier, these goods were not even available for consumption by the general population. It is amazing that in such a short period of time, both came into existence and became available to even the poor, and in such great numbers.

In brief, free and open markets are necessary but not sufficient conditions for an inventive, dynamic economy. They are not the essence of capitalism, but an indispensable handmaid to it.

Free Societies Are Inherently Fragile

Some observers have asked whether, for certain aspiring nations, China's political economy now serves as a better model than democratic capitalism. The question is an empirical one to be settled by observable evidence.

As a matter of principle, the Chinese leadership is betting on the possibility of sustaining economic liberty without political liberties. It is currently willing to risk its future without the checks and balances built into a republican form of democracy. I judge that this project will not be successful. Once there are a sufficient number of successful entrepreneurs, they will see that in important respects they are smarter and larger in mental horizon than the party commissars. They will resent the errors made by apparatchiks. They will demand their own representation in national decisions—that is, representative government with its checks and balances. I may be wrong about this, but empirical experience will be decisive.

Notwithstanding what happens in China, the sad fact is that almost everywhere in the world today, systems properly called capitalist *and* democratic are facing grave difficulties. It cannot be supposed that human beings always love liberty. Free persons must meet the burdens of personal responsibility, and for some, that responsibility is too onerous. If I may paraphrase Dostoevsky: "When people cry out for liberty, give it to them—in fifteen minutes they will give it back." For most of history, humans have been remarkably unrebellious under tyranny. Meet their simplest appetites, and why should they take up irksome responsibilities?

So it is today. Not all human beings desire to be economically free; for if they are free, they are obligated to bear responsibility for their own welfare. Of course, of course, there is always some percentage of the population who are too old or too young, too ill or too disabled, to carry their own weight in economic responsibility. There will always be some people who rightly depend upon the help of others. By its own moral identity, any honest Jewish, Christian, or even secular humanist society must come to their aid.

Furthermore, in practical terms it is necessary to distribute some portion of this aid through federal and local governments, given that American society has become so mobile, with so many Americans now separated from the families and friends who in earlier generations provided the informal safety nets that many relied on in old age and other times of need. Also, as John Paul II pointed out in

Centesimus Annus, there are huge drawbacks in entrusting such welfare exclusively to the administrative state (as he called modern state systems).[19] Such a state is a highly flawed instrument for helping the poor. For one thing, it tends to treat them (indeed, by legal requirements of equal protection, *must* treat them) as interchangeable units of the citizenry, and too often this means impersonally. That is, the state must treat them as clients rather than as full-fledged, responsible persons with their own unique backgrounds, needs, and aspirations.

The big argument in these matters is not *whether* the poor must be helped. It is not even whether the federal government plays a necessary role in providing that assistance. The answer to both those questions is *yes*.

The big argument, rather, is about how: by what means and by what methods best to do this. Some among us do not trust private efforts, private business, corporations, or even individuals and civic associations to bring sufficient care to the able-bodied poor. Instead, they prefer to trust government to do so, even if only by borrowing money, for which task they pledge the obligations of their children and their grandchildren. Such persons may be models of compassion, but their generosity is dubious when they do not resolve to pay for their own moral preening.

Meanwhile, others hold that entrusting too much care for the able-bodied to the administrative state brings many evils in its train and almost guarantees the creation of more dependency, unhappiness, and loss of dignity. Of course, those holding this view tend to believe that there are two kinds of personal dignity. One is a birthright coming from nature or from the Creator, as the Declaration of Independence states. The other, earned dignity, comes only from personal accomplishment. In tension with this position, some feel that one's dignity is better preserved if one does not have to suffer the humiliation of turning to and depending on the personal kindness of others. Still, many believe that turning to others for mutual help, and bearing mutual responsibilities, is a two-way street. The sick and the disabled, the very young and very old are more dependent than the fit and the able. But even the latter depend on each other in many ways. We each earn dignity by mutually pitching in, and no able-bodied person should be just a taker. To become so is to lose dignity in one's own eyes, not just in the eyes of others. When the Clinton welfare reforms obliged receivers also to pitch in and work, many reports noted the higher morale of those receiving government aid, who were now proud of their own contributions.[2]

More than that, the society of dependency often breeds dangerous corruption, a kind of serfdom. In exchange for their liberty, many are cared for as passive animals: fed, sheltered, herded about. It is unfortunate that the administrative state, given excessive power and responsibility, crowds out the personal help given by one family to another and by churches and other private organizations, as well as the activation of the many resources of responsible neighbors together, which occurs in vibrant civil societies. In proportion as the state grows fat, civil society more and more shrivels, loses its muscle—and energy and motivation. On the other side, the belly of the power-seeking state grows bloated from the dependency of more and more citizens. The more new needs that can be satisfied by the state, the greater its power swells. And so do its expenses, that is, its debts.

In truth, all seem to agree that one of the great moral imperatives of our time is to help the last remaining billion poor persons today to free themselves from poverty. Some tend to think that this help must be done mostly through the state because no one else will do it. Others think the best way is to set up a beneficent circle through which creative work generates new wealth from the bottom of society up, and such wealth is again invested in new enterprises and new industries. Systems characterized by almost universal opportunity for beginners and steady upward mobility win the undying gratitude of those fortunate enough to inhabit them. These lucky ones know that they win rewards out of proportion to their effort. In the old country, my grandfather thought, he could have worked far harder than in the United States, but still won fewer rewards. He attributed the greater rewards he received here to the new system he found here, more than to himself.

Some do not trust that large corporations or even small businesses will help the poor. They don't trust the profit motive. They understand the motive of self-interest as a vice, not as a discipline. They don't recognize that "self-interest" is a morally neutral word. Sometimes it stands for something transcendently good: "For what shall it profit a man, if he shall gain the whole world, and lose his own soul?"[21] It is more in our self-interest to love our neighbor as ourselves and to love God above all. It is in our interest to ask God to make us more holy. Some self-interests are evil, some are neutral, and some are very good.

While some put their trust in programs of the state, others among us think that the fastest way to raise up the poor is to reform most existing systems, so as to align institutions with the actual workings of human nature. Such reform would include new laws that favor persons who want to improve the condition of their own families and that secure for the children of hardworking parents advantages that in their early poverty they did not themselves enjoy. These are not evil motives, not even selfish motives, for they entail great personal sacrifices. Systems that do not move their populations from poverty to decent wealth in less than a generation are flawed and ought to be reformed. Moreover, this is a realistic hope. Dozens of nations from around the world have profoundly reformed their systems and bettered the daily lot of their citizens in a relatively short time.

Consider South Korea, Singapore, Hong Kong, and Taiwan after, say, 1960. Even India and Bangladesh have become net exporters of food and manufactured goods, and the average age of mortality in each has risen sharply and impressively.[22] (The average age of mortality is one of the best indices of human progress, for it measures what is not solely material.) The progress one sees in Poland, Slovakia, and the Czech Republic since 1989 is nothing short of stunning.[23] And it is not only material progress; it is progress in smiling and joy, and in walking down the street with a sense of purpose, rather than the downcast, lowered-head lassitude of the Soviet era.

One thing leaders in poor nations do well to avoid: they should not tie their people's hopes to the flag of equality. As Pope Leo XIII wrote in his great letter to the world *Rerum Novarum* (1891), to insist that humans be equal—each one so unique and different even from their brothers and sisters—is futile, evil, and destructive of the common good.[24] Similarly, the American founders, notably Benjamin Franklin and Thomas Jefferson, studied what had made republics in history so frequently fail. They diagnosed the seed of such self-destruction in envy, which begins to grow when one part of a society is divided against another: one leading family against another, one part of a city against another, one ethnic group against another, the poor against the rich and vice versa.[25] Envy is the most insidious enemy of the common good, for it works always under disguise. It does not call itself envy. It calls itself equality or fairness.

Political leaders who have led their people under the flag of equality have come to be despised as liars and nincompoops, and held up as laughingstocks. For no scheme can make people equal who are not alike in talent, spirit, hard work, a drive to excel, or the desire to live free, responsible for one's own destiny, and self-directed. The banner of equality cannot inspire people to work, to save, and to leverage self-denial in the present in order to gain their own better condition in the future. Rather, it incites the many against the so-called 1-percenters. A very high social price will one day be paid for group envy. No regime is more fragile, more in mortal danger, than a society divided against itself, one part at war with another.

Of course, to defeat envy, a society must be structured in a nontraditional way. It must open up many avenues to upward mobility, variously suited to diverse talents and personal drives. It must encourage persons to pursue their own sense of self-fulfillment (their happiness) in their own way. For example, my father turned down offers of higher-paying jobs in order to spend more time with his family, rather than spending weeks on the road in a managerial post. People are happiest who do not compare their own status with that of others, but compare where they are in light of their own life-goals.

Biblical Roots

On the ceiling of the Sistine Chapel in the Vatican is a great fresco of the creation of Adam by the energy emanating from the finger of the Creator. If you notice closely, there is a violet shadow behind the head of the Creator, in the shape of a man's cranium. The capacity of the human cranium for creative energy is one way in which Adam and Eve are made in the image of their Creator.

Reflect on this a little: Many of the inspirations of the threefold system of political economy derive from evangelical inspirations such as personal creativity, personal responsibility, freedom, the love for community through association and mutual cooperation, the aim of bettering the condition of every person on earth, the cultivation of the rule of law, respect for the natural rights of others, the preference of persuasion by reason rather than by coercion, a powerful sense of the sinful drag on human souls and the need for checks against these. All these imperatives spring from the Bible. (It is a good exercise to find the biblical texts that put these drives within us into motion.) That is why capitalism—and societies free not only in their economic system but also in their polity and their culture—have arisen with more energy and less friction in areas where Jewish and Christian traditions are strong. Most often these evangelical impulsions have appeared in such areas first.

When the future Pope John Paul II was still a young bishop at the

Second Vatican Council, he was writing his great work of philosophy, *The Acting Person*.[26] How, he asked, does a person differ from a dog, or stone, or rosebush? The human person is able to reflect back on the deeds of his life and to pass judgment on them. She may repent of some and wish to strengthen others in herself. Similarly, she is capable of (and needs) insight into the many possible courses her future life might follow, in order to choose among them. These capacities for insight, reflection, and decision regarding one's past and future allow one to shape one's own identity. They impart a dignity based on unavoidable human responsibilities, well or ill met. Note, too, that these capacities for insight and decision are crucial for the virtues of creativity and enterprise. One of the ways in which humans are made in the image of God is the ability to use their own capacity for inventiveness to discern the unmet needs of humans and a way to meet them (often a new and unprecedented way). This is the chief road to economic creativity and human progress.

Some who speak from a Christian perspective still think that mildly socialist ideas such as anti-individualism, collectivist projects, income equality, and a vision of full state welfare benefits are closer to the mandate of the gospel than to democratic capitalist institutions. Some of the earliest American settlers from Europe, the first Pilgrims in Massachusetts, also thought so, until by the end of the first winter they nearly all starved to death. Our forebears learned the practical effects of collectivist methods: No one in a commune feels a personal motive to stay up at night with a sick cow (someone else will do it, I'm too tired), and the hardest workers who observe the loafers and free-riders will begin to reduce their own labors.

Personal responsibility matters. Incentives matter. Personal labor and earning your own bread by the sweat of your brow matter (Genesis 3:19). Personal responsibility for one's own dependents and for needy neighbors matters. Biblical religion lays heavy duties on responsible persons. As Franklin D. Roosevelt stressed in his 1935

State of the Union address, state welfare systems must avoid the danger that welfare corrupts, destroys incentives, and encourages attitudes of laziness and irresponsibility: "The lessons of history, confirmed by the evidence immediately before me, show conclusively that continued dependence upon relief induces a spiritual disintegration fundamentally destructive to the national fiber. To dole our relief in this way is to administer a narcotic, a subtle destroyer of the human spirit."[27]

Persons struck by sudden misfortune (a divorce, say, or the abrupt loss of a job, or a surprise diagnosis of an incurable disease, or an incapacitating automobile accident) often do need a helping hand. Given that hand, many are back up on their feet in just a year or two, living without government help, but with plenty of help from their families, churches, and many associations. Governmental aid is often vital. But it does carry a danger. The love of God is personal, right in the eyes and heart; but government must obey rules and regulations with a certain impersonality as if dealing with a client. Government help can strip persons of their dignity as free and responsible achievers with a sense of their own accomplishments.

In addition, too many people seem not to notice that the vices of self-interest, which they detect everywhere else, are always at play in government work. Governments fail at many tasks; and when they do, officials are tempted to ask for more money and more employees and find it easier just to take over personal responsibilities rather than allow their clients the chance to earn personal satisfaction from their successes.

Many observers look down on the results of traditionalist, static market systems, as they should. But they wrongly assume that these are capitalist systems, when they are quite precapitalist. Certain tests help mark the difference. In precapitalist systems, there is little movement among socio-economic ranks, little downward mobility among the traditionally privileged class, too little news of success stories formed by the upward push of creative and insightful persons among the formerly poor. But the most important indicator of the economic progress in any nation is its rate of new business formations, this year as compared to last. Since some 65 percent of new jobs (in most places) arise from the success of new small businesses,[28] a high rate of business start-ups is quite promising for growth from the bottom up. By contrast, a low rate of business start-ups bodes ill.

Many of us think that our ideas about how to raise the poor out of poverty work a lot better than the alternatives. Here are the practical principles we adhere to: Begin with the story of Creation and apply it to the economic order. Hold to a vision of the creation of wealth for all nations, not just for a few individuals. Be open to the rare and powerful talents that God has implanted among the poorest among us. Count it the aim of the good economy and the good polity to struggle until every single able-bodied man and woman within their jurisdiction (and also abroad) is raised out of poverty.

Accomplish these aims by doing the following: (1) Make the legal incorporation of economic entities low-cost, quick, and bribe-free. (2) Put in place institutions that support economic activism and solidarity among all human persons, the rich, the middle-class, and the poor. Chief among these are institutions that lend money to new small business entrepreneurs, who sometimes need only micro-loans, and lend at low rates for sufficient periods of time. When such institutions also lend expert advice to fledgling start-ups, they increase the chances of recovering their loans through the success of those they mean to help. Through such institutions in Silicon Valley, the first primitive Apple computer invented in a garage by two college dropouts drew staying power. Eventually their work won them funds to put up a factory up-to-date enough to build scores of thousands of new computers and get them to market. Among the poor who have no capital, the ability to borrow money to nurture small businesses through their rocky beginnings is a godsend. (3)

Develop an educational system that prepares youngsters to start their own businesses, to think creatively about their economic future, and to learn techniques of success in economic activities. Among the poorest of the poor, God's outreaching fingers have spread many creative minds, vivid imaginations, and willing and hardworking hands.

But for the poor to get their inventions and discoveries into the hands of all who might benefit from them takes many institutions: some for setting up sound business plans, some for venture capital, some for timely professional advice and guidance. The ensemble of all those institutions that support creative and inventive mind is what we mean by capitalism rightly understood. These include a polity and a culture that nourish the moral habits that create wealth rather than merely consume it, and that instill ambition, discipline, and self-denial for the sake of future good, rather than merely indulging in what one receives from others.

As the former motto of Amsterdam put it, *Commercium et Pax*. Commerce needs and encourages peace. It does so through its reliance on and encouragement of the rule of law. Without wise laws, human behaviors are erratic, not to say wild and unpredictable. In such circumstances commerce cannot prosper. Indeed, in extensive commerce under the rule of law, St. Ephrem of Syria (c. 306-373) and other Church fathers saw the dependence of one country upon others, each having different products, each being indispensable to one another. They saw in such global commerce a worldly illustration of the unity of the human race and how the mystical body of Christ works, each distinctive part contributing to the others.[29]

Conclusion

Whether in evangelical, practical, or intellectual terms, the combination of the three systems in one—the democratic republic, a creative and dynamic economy, and an open, free, and pluralistic culture—has a proven modern record surpassed by none in raising up the poor. It is a system born of Judaism and Christianity and is most congenial to them. It generates unparalleled progress in every sphere from medicine to the cultivation of beauty, the spread of the rule of law, the protection of natural rights, and the search for justice for all.

Nothing says, however, that such a system, which depends on good habits of the heart, cannot pass into the darkness of human history like a self-destructing comet, soon to burn out. That outcome depends on each succeeding generation. The free society is the most fragile of all societies, because any one generation can become oblivious to its multiple living principles, live unworthily of them, hand over the keys, and walk out into darkness.

Only one generation is required. Yet in practice the downward slide usually begins three or four generations earlier than the final collapse. Our own generation sometimes seems to be hurtling future generations downward. Our system can quickly destroy itself. A lasting civilization is either moral or self-destructive.

We have hardly begun to address the rapid decline in the moral ecology of world culture. Many evils and much self-destructive behavior run rampant on earth. This is the new frontier of political economy: the culture in which the free society thrives or destroys itself.

We are very far from having built the kingdom of God on earth. But we have dramatically reduced poverty, shown ways to build institutions that respect human rights and liberties, virtually eliminated famines, found ways to prevent and remedy diseases, dramatically increased the longevity of peoples everywhere, and come to include more and more persons in the "circle of exchange," to the extent that some people even speak of global advancement. But that, too, has not yet been achieved in full. There still remain about a billion persons on earth not yet included.

To summarize: God, whom we know as that unique form of love, *Caritas*, freely created human beings in this universe and directed them to build up the city of *Caritas*: "Thy kingdom come . . . in earth, as it is in heaven."[31] As William Penn pointed out, if God created the world for friendship, then it must be a world ruled by free choice.[32] God wanted the love of free women and free men, not by coercion. The Lord also made us in his image, that is, to be creative. And true love is realistic about human weaknesses and failings. This world is a world of sinners, and therefore it is right to devise divisions of power, so that each power is checked and balanced by another. Finally, the Lord says, "Go . . . teach all nations,"[33] and thus the perspective of love must be planetary in scope and must look to the welfare of all nations and all persons within them.

These are realities about which Judaism and Christianity are quite eloquent. These are the originating impulses from which eventually, only about two centuries ago, the mind-centered system of invention and enterprise began to break out in one place after another on earth.

NOTES

[1] Michael Novak, *The Spirit of Democratic Capitalism* (New York: Simon & Schuster, 1982).

[2] "Capitalism." http://www.merriam-webster.com/dictionary/capitalism (accessed August 21, 2014).

[3] See Karl Marx, *Capital: A Critique of Political Economy, Vol. 1, Part 1 - The Process of Capitalist Production*, ed. Friedrich Engels (1867; New York: Cosimo, 2007), 708-709.

[4] See Jerry Muller, *Adam Smith in His Time and Ours: Designing the Decent Society* (New York: The Free Press, 1993), 60, 68, 72, 148, 160.

[5] See Adam Smith, *An Inquiry into the Nature and Causes of the Wealth of Nations* (1776; New York: Cosimo, 2007), 9-11.

[6] Source: http://visualizingeconomics.com/blog/2007/11/11/two-thousand-years-of-growth-world-income-population (accessed August 20, 2014).

[7] Adam Smith, *An Inquiry into the Nature and Causes of the Wealth of Nations*, 466.

[8] See Alexis de Tocqueville, *Democracy in America*, vol. 1, tr. Henry Reeve. http://www.gutenberg.org/files/815/815-h/815-h.htm (accessed August 21, 2014); *Democracy in America*, vol. 2, tr. Henry Reeve. http://www.gutenberg.org/files/816/816-h/816-h.htm (accessed August 21, 2014).

[9] For example, see Alexander Hamilton, *The Federalist*, no. 9. http://www.constitution.org/fed/federa09.htm (accessed August 21, 2014).

[10] The term "Fabian socialism" refers to a form of socialism promoted by members of the Fabian Society, founded in London in the late nineteenth century. As distinct from then-contemporary radical communist movements that favored socialist goals by means of revolution and even anarchy, Fabians argued for the gradual evolution of socialism through state-administered institutions and programs.

[11] The "demogrant" program was a proposal by 1972 presidential candidate George McGovern that the federal government give $1000 to each citizen. The proposal was widely discredited as pandering, and McGovern abandoned it.

[12] "Stagflation," from *stagnation* plus *inflation*, describes the combination of the conditions of high inflation and unemployment rates, together with low economic growth.

[13] James Madison, *The Federalist*, no. 14. http://www.constitution.org/fed/federa14.htm (accessed August 21, 2014).

[14] "Before then [the adoption of the United States Constitution], any man might

instantly use what another had invented; so that the inventor had no special advantage from his own invention. The patent system changed this; secured to the inventor, for a limited time, the exclusive use of his invention; and thereby added the fuel of interest to the fire of genius, in the discovery and production of new and useful things." Abraham Lincoln, *Second Lecture on Discoveries and Inventions* (February 11, 1859). http://www.abrahamlincolnonline.org/lincoln/speeches/discoveries.htm (accessed August 21, 2014).

[15] Pope John Paul II, *Centesimus Annus*, §25. http://www.vatican.va/holy_father/john_paul_ii/encyclicals/documents/hf_jp-ii_enc_01051991_centesimus-annus_en.html (accessed August 21, 2014).

[16] Pope John Paul II, *Centesimus Annus*, §32. http://www.vatican.va/holy_father/john_paul_ii/encyclicals/documents/hf_jp-ii_enc_01051991_centesimus-annus_en.html (accessed August 21, 2014).

[17] Robert Rector and Rachel Sheffield, "Air Conditioning, Cable TV, and an Xbox: What is Poverty in the United States Today?" The Heritage Foundation (July 19, 2011). http://www.heritage.org/research/reports/2011/07/what-is-poverty (accessed August 21, 2014).

[18] See *The Brothers Karamazov*, chapter 5, "The Grand Inquisitor." http://www.gutenberg.org/ebooks/8578 (accessed August 21, 2014).

[19] Pope John Paul II, *Centesimus Annus*, §48. http://www.vatican.va/holy_father/john_paul_ii/encyclicals/documents/hf_jp-ii_enc_01051991_centesimus-annus_en.html (accessed August 21, 2014).

[20] For example, see Ann Tickamyer, Debra Henderson, and Barry Tadlock, "Does Welfare Reform Work in Rural America? A 7-Year Follow-up." www.ukcpr.org/Publications/DP2007-06.pdf (accessed August 21, 2014).

[21] Matthew 8:36 (KJV).

[22] See "Bangladesh – Life Expectancy at Birth," Index Mundi, http://www.indexmundi.com/facts/bangladesh/life-expectancy-at-birth (accessed August 21, 2014); "India – Life Expectancy at Birth," Index Mundi, http://www.indexmundi.com/facts/india/life-expectancy-at-birth (accessed August 21, 2014).

[23] See "Economic Transformation in Poland after 1989," http://www.investin-poland.pl/eng/index.php?option=content&task=view&id=10&Itemid=32 (accessed August 21, 2014); "2014 Index of Economic Freedom," http://www.heritage.org/index/country/slovakia (accessed August 21, 2014); "Development of Czech Economy," http://www.czech.cz/en/Business/Economic-facts/Development-of-Czech-economy (accessed August 21, 2014).

[24] See Pope Leo XIII, *Rerum Novarum*, §§15-18. http://www.vatican.va/holy_father/leo_xiii/encyclicals/documents/hf_l-xiii_enc_15051891_rerum-novarum_en.html (accessed August 21, 2014).

[25] See, for example, John Jay, *The Federalist*, no. 5. http://www.constitution.org/fed/federa05.htm (accessed August 21, 2014).

[26] Pope John Paul II, *The Acting Person: A Contribution to Phenomenological Anthropology*, ed. and tr. Anna-Teresa Tymieniecka (1969; Dordrecht: D. Reidel Publishing Company, 1979).

[27] Franklin D. Roosevelt, "State of the Union Address of 1935." http://www.albany.edu/faculty/gz580/his101/su35fdr.html (accessed August 21, 2014).

[28] Jason Nazaar, "16 Surprising Statistics about Small Businesses," Forbes (September 9, 2013). http://www.forbes.com/sites/jasonnazar/2013/09/09/16-surprising-statistics-about-small-businesses/ (accessed August 21, 2014).

[29] See Michael Novak and Paul Barry Clarke, "Business," in *Dictionary of Ethics, Theology and Society*, ed. Paul Barry Clarke and Andrew Linzey (New York: Routledge, 1996), 96-99.

[30] Pope John Paul II, *Centesimus Annus*, §34. http://www.vatican.va/holy_father/john_paul_ii/encyclicals/documents/hf_jp-ii_enc_01051991_centesimus-annus_en.html (accessed August 21, 2014).

[31] Matthew 6:10 (KJV).

[32] See William Penn, "Some Fruits of Solitude in Reflection and Maxims," no. 107. http://www.fordham.edu/halsall/mod/1682penn-solitude.asp (accessed August 21, 2014).

[33] Matthew 28:19 (KJV).

About The Institute for Faith, Work & Economics

IFWE is a Christian research organization committed to promoting biblical principles that help Christians thrive in the workplace for the glory of God, the common good and the advancement of God's kingdom. IFWE conducts and translates high-level theological and economic research into practical resources that will help Christians integrate their faith in the workplace and become better stewards of all that God has given them. For more information, visit www.tifwe.org.

Made in the USA
Middletown, DE
15 February 2022